The Wisdom of Solomon

Copyright © 2016 Beloved Publishing

Beloved Publishing

Pickerington, Ohio

www.BelovedPublishing.com - "Discover a Classic"

Printed in the United States of America

First edition

ISBN: 1631741543

Wis.1

[1] Love righteousness, ye that be judges of the earth: think of the Lord with a good (heart,) and in simplicity of heart seek him.

[2] For he will be found of them that tempt him not; and sheweth himself unto such as do not distrust him.

[3] For froward thoughts separate from God: and his power, when it is tried, reproveth the unwise.

[4] For into a malicious soul wisdom shall not enter; nor dwell in the body that is subject unto sin.

[5] For the holy spirit of discipline will flee deceit, and remove from thoughts that are without understanding, and will not abide when unrighteousness cometh in.

[6] For wisdom is a loving spirit; and will not acquit a blasphemer of his words: for God is witness of his reins, and a true beholder of his heart, and a hearer of his tongue.

[7] For the Spirit of the Lord filleth the world: and that which containeth all things hath knowledge of the voice.

[8] Therefore he that speaketh unrighteous things cannot be hid: neither shall vengeance, when it punisheth, pass by him.

[9] For inquisition shall be made into the counsels of the ungodly: and the sound of his

words shall come unto the Lord for the manifestation of his wicked deeds.

[10] For the ear of jealousy heareth all things: and the noise of murmurings is not hid.

[11] Therefore beware of murmuring, which is unprofitable; and refrain your tongue from backbiting: for there is no word so secret, that shall go for nought: and the mouth that belieth slayeth the soul.

[12] Seek not death in the error of your life: and pull not upon yourselves destruction with the works of your hands.

[13] For God made not death: neither hath he pleasure in the destruction of the living.

[14] For he created all things, that they might have their being: and the generations of the world were healthful; and there is no poison of destruction in them, nor the kingdom of death upon the earth:

[15] (For righteousness is immortal:)

[16] But ungodly men with their works and words called it to them: for when they thought to have it their friend, they consumed to nought, and made a covenant with it, because they are worthy to take part with it.

Wis.2

[1] For the ungodly said, reasoning with themselves, but not aright, Our life is short and tedious, and in the death of a man there is no remedy: neither was there any man known to have returned from the grave.

[2] For we are born at all adventure: and we shall be hereafter as though we had never been: for the breath in our nostrils is as smoke, and a little spark in the moving of our heart:

[3] Which being extinguished, our body shall be turned into ashes, and our spirit shall vanish as the soft air,

[4] And our name shall be forgotten in time, and no man shall have our works in remembrance, and our life shall pass away as the trace of a cloud, and shall be dispersed as a mist, that is driven away with the beams of the sun, and overcome with the heat thereof.

[5] For our time is a very shadow that passeth away; and after our end there is no returning: for it is fast sealed, so that no man cometh again.

[6] Come on therefore, let us enjoy the good things that are present: and let us speedily use the creatures like as in youth.

[7] Let us fill ourselves with costly wine and ointments: and let no flower of the spring pass by us:

[8] Let us crown ourselves with rosebuds, before they be withered:

[9] Let none of us go without his part of our voluptuousness: let us leave tokens of our joyfulness in every place: for this is our portion, and our lot is this.

[10] Let us oppress the poor righteous man, let us not spare the widow, nor reverence the ancient gray hairs of the aged.

[11] Let our strength be the law of justice: for that which is feeble is found to be nothing worth.

[12] Therefore let us lie in wait for the righteous; because he is not for our turn, and he is clean contrary to our doings: he upbraideth us with our offending the law, and objecteth to our infamy the transgressions of our education.

[13] He professeth to have the knowledge of God: and he calleth himself the child of the Lord.

[14] He was made to reprove our thoughts.

[15] He is grievous unto us even to behold: for his life is not like other men's, his ways are of another fashion.

[16] We are esteemed of him as counterfeits: he abstaineth from our ways as from filthiness: he pronounceth the end of the just to be blessed, and maketh his boast that God is his father.

[17] Let us see if his words be true: and let us prove what shall happen in the end of him.

[18] For if the just man be the son of God, he will help him, and deliver him from the hand of his enemies.

[19] Let us examine him with despitefulness and torture, that we may know his meekness, and prove his patience.

[20] Let us condemn him with a shameful death: for by his own saying he shall be respected.

[21] Such things they did imagine, and were deceived: for their own wickedness hath blinded them.

[22] As for the mysteries of God, they kn ew them not: neither hoped they for the wages of righteousness, nor discerned a reward for blameless souls.

[23] For God created man to be immortal, and made him to be an image of his own eternity.

[24] Nevertheless through envy of the devil came death into the world: and they that do hold of his side do find it.

Wis.3

[1] But the souls of the righteous are in the hand of God, and there shall no torment touch them.

[2] In the sight of the unwise they seemed to die: and their departure is taken for misery,

[3] And their going from us to be utter destruction: but they are in peace.

[4] For though they be punished in the sight of men, yet is their hope full of immortality.

[5] And having been a little chastised, they shall be greatly rewarded: for God proved them, and found them worthy for himself.

[6] As gold in the furnace hath he tried them, and received them as a burnt offering.

[7] And in the time of their visitation they shall shine, and run to and fro like sparks among the stubble.

[8] They shall judge the nations, and have dominion over the people, and their Lord shall reign for ever.

[9] They that put their trust in him shall understand the truth: and such as be faithful in love shall abide with him: for grace and mercy is to his saints, and he hath care for his elect.

[10] But the ungodly shall be punished according to their own imaginations, which have neglected the righteous, and forsaken the Lord.

[11] For whoso despiseth wisdom and nurture, he is miserable, and their hope is vain, their labours unfruitful, and their works unprofitable:

[12] Their wives are foolish, and their children wicked:

[13] Their offspring is cursed. Wherefore blessed is the barren that is undefiled, which hath not known the sinful bed: she shall have fruit in the visitation of souls.

[14] And blessed is the eunuch, which with his hands hath wrought no iniquity, nor imagined wicked things against God: for unto him shall be given the special gift of faith, and an inheritance in the temple of the Lord more acceptable to his mind.

[15] For glorious is the fruit of good labours: and the root of wisdom shall never fall away.

[16] As for the children of adulterers, they shall not come to their perfection, and the seed of an unrighteous bed shall be rooted out.

[17] For though they live long, yet shall they be nothing regarded: and their last age shall be without honour.

[18] Or, if they die quickly, they have no hope, neither comfort in the day of trial.

[19] For horrible is the end of the unrighteous generation.

Wis.4

[1] Better it is to have no children, and to have virtue: for the memorial thereof is immortal: because it is known with God, and with men.

[2] When it is present, men take example at it; and when it is gone, they desire it: it weareth a crown, and triumpheth for ever, having gotten the victory, striving for undefiled rewards.

[3] But the multiplying brood of the ungodly shall not thrive, nor take deep rooting from bastard slips, nor lay any fast foundation.

[4] For though they flourish in branches for a time; yet standing not last, they shall be shaken with the wind, and through the force of winds they shall be rooted out.

[5] The imperfect branches shall be broken off, their fruit unprofitable, not ripe to eat, yea, meet for nothing.

[6] For children begotten of unlawful beds are witnesses of wickedness against their parents in their trial.

[7] But though the righteous be prevented with death, yet shall he be in rest.

[8] For honourable age is not that which standeth in length of time, nor that is measured by number of years.

[9] But wisdom is the gray hair unto men, and an unspotted life is old age.

[10] He pleased God, and was beloved of him: so that living among sinners he was translated.

[11] Yea speedily was he taken away, lest that wickedness should alter his understanding, or deceit beguile his soul.

[12] For the bewitching of naughtiness doth obscure things that are honest; and the wandering of concupiscence doth undermine the simple mind.

[13] He, being made perfect in a short time, fulfilled a long time:

[14] For his soul pleased the Lord: therefore hasted he to take him away from among the wicked.

[15] This the people saw, and understood it not, neither laid they up this in their minds, That his grace and mercy is with his saints, and that he hath respect unto his chosen.

[16] Thus the righteous that is dead shall condemn the ungodly which are living; and youth that is soon perfected the many years and old age of the unrighteous.

[17] For they shall see the end of the wise, and shall not understand what God in his counsel hath decreed of him, and to what end the Lord hath set him in safety.

[18] They shall see him, and despise him; but God shall laugh them to scorn: and they shall hereafter be a vile carcase, and a reproach among the dead for evermore.

[19] For he shall rend them, and cast them down headlong, that they shall be speechless; and he shall shake them from the foundation; and they shall be utterly laid waste, and be in sorrow; and their memorial shall perish.

[20] And when they cast up the accounts of their sins, they shall come with fear: and their own iniquities shall convince them to their face.

Wis.5

[1] Then shall the righteous man stand in great boldness before the face of such as have afflicted him, and made no account of his labours.

[2] When they see it, they shall be troubled with terrible fear, and shall be amazed at the strangeness of his salvation, so far beyond all that they looked for.

[3] And they repenting and groaning for anguish of spirit shall say within themselves, This was he, whom we had sometimes in derision, and a proverb of reproach:

[4] We fools accounted his life madness, and his end to be without honour:

[5] How is he numbered among the children of God, and his lot is among the saints!

[6] Therefore have we erred from the way of truth, and the light of righteousness hath not shined unto us, and the sun of righteousness rose not upon us.

[7] We wearied ourselves in the way of wickedness and destruction: yea, we have gone through deserts, where there lay no way: but as for the way of the Lord, we have not known it.

[8] What hath pride profited us? or what good hath riches with our vaunting brought us?

[9] All those things are passed away like a shadow, and as a post that hasted by;

[10] And as a ship that passeth over the waves of the water, which when it is gone by, the trace thereof cannot be found, neither the pathway of the keel in the waves;

[11] Or as when a bird hath flown through the air, there is no token of her way to be found, but the light air being beaten with the stroke of her wings and parted with the violent noise and motion of them, is passed through, and therein afterwards no sign where she went is to be found;

[12] Or like as when an arrow is shot at a mark, it parteth the air, which immediately cometh together again, so that a man cannot know where it went through:

[13] Even so we in like manner, as soon as we were born, began to draw to our end, and had no sign of virtue to shew; but were consumed in our own wickedness.

[14] For the hope of the Godly is like dust that is blown away with the wind; like a thin froth that is driven away with the storm; like as the smoke which is dispersed here and there with a tempest, and passeth away as the remembrance of a guest that tarrieth but a day.

[15] But the righteous live for evermore; their reward also is with the Lord, and the care of them is with the most High.

[16] Therefore shall they receive a glorious kingdom, and a beautiful crown from the

Lord's hand: for with his right hand shall he cover them, and with his arm shall he protect them.

[17] He shall take to him his jealousy for complete armour, and make the creature his weapon for the revenge of his enemies.

[18] He shall put on righteousness as a breastplate, and true judgment instead of an helmet.

[19] He shall take holiness for an invincible shield.

[20] His severe wrath shall he sharpen for a sword, and the world shall fight with him against the unwise.

[21] Then shall the right aiming thunderbolts go abroad; and from the clouds, as from a well drawn bow, shall they fly to the mark.

[22] And hailstones full of wrath shall be cast as out of a stone bow, and the water of the sea shall rage against them, and the floods shall cruelly drown them.

[23] Yea, a mighty wind shall stand up against them, and like a storm shall blow them away: thus iniquity shall lay waste the whole earth, and ill dealing shall overthrow the thrones of the mighty.

Wis.6

[1] Hear therefore, O ye kings, and understand; learn, ye that be judges of the ends of the earth.

[2] Give ear, ye that rule the people, and glory in the multitude of nations.

[3] For power is given you of the Lord, and sovereignty from the Highest, who shall try your works, and search out your counsels.

[4] Because, being ministers of his kingdom, ye have not judged aright, nor kept the law, nor walked after the counsel of God;

[5] Horribly and speedily shall he come upon you: for a sharp judgment shall be to them that be in high places.

[6] For mercy will soon pardon the meanest: but mighty men shall be mightily tormented.

[7] For he which is Lord over all shall fear no man's person, neither shall he stand in awe of any man's greatness: for he hath made the small and great, and careth for all alike.

[8] But a sore trial shall come upon the mighty.

[9] Unto you therefore, O kings, do I speak, that ye may learn wisdom, and not fall away.

[10] For they that keep holiness holily shall be judged holy: and they that have learned such things shall find what to answer.

[11] Wherefore set your affection upon my words; desire them, and ye shall be instructed.

[12] Wisdom is glorious, and never fadeth away: yea, she is easily seen of them that love her, and found of such as seek her.

[13] She preventeth them that desire her, in making herself first known unto them.

[14] Whoso seeketh her early shall have no great travail: for he shall find her sitting at his doors.

[15] To think therefore upon her is perfection of wisdom: and whoso watcheth for her shall quickly be without care.

[16] For she goeth about seeking such as are worthy of her, sheweth herself favourably unto them in the ways, and meeteth them in every thought.

[17] For the very true beginning of her is the desire of discipline; and the care of discipline is love;

[18] And love is the keeping of her laws; and the giving heed unto her laws is the assurance of incorruption;

[19] And incorruption maketh us near unto God:

[20] Therefore the desire of wisdom bringeth to a kingdom.

[21] If your delight be then in thrones and sceptres, O ye kings of the people, honour wisdom, that ye may reign for evermore.

[22] As for wisdom, what she is, and how she came up, I will tell you, and will not hide mysteries from you: but will seek her out from

the beginning of her nativity, and bring the knowledge of her into light, and will not pass over the truth.

[23] Neither will I go with consuming envy; for such a man shall have no fellowship with wisdom.

[24] But the multitude of the wise is the welfare of the world: and a wise king is the upholding of the people.

[25] Receive therefore instruction through my words, and it shall do you good.

Wis.7

[1] I myself also am a mortal man, like to all, and the offspring of him that was first made of the earth,

[2] And in my mother's womb was fashioned to be flesh in the time of ten months, being compacted in blood, of the seed of man, and the pleasure that came with sleep.

[3] And when I was born, I drew in the common air, and fell upon the earth, which is of like nature, and the first voice which I uttered was crying, as all others do.

[4] I was nursed in swaddling clothes, and that with cares.

[5] For there is no king that had any other beginning of birth.

[6] For all men have one entrance into life, and the like going out.

[7] Wherefore I prayed, and understanding was given me: I called upon God, and the spirit of wisdom came to me.

[8] I preferred her before sceptres and thrones, and esteemed riches nothing in comparison of her.

[9] Neither compared I unto her any precious stone, because all gold in respect of her is as a little sand, and silver shall be counted as clay before her.

[10] I loved her above health and beauty, and chose to have her instead of light: for the light that cometh from her never goeth out.

[11] All good things together came to me with her, and innumerable riches in her hands.

[12] And I rejoiced in them all, because wisdom goeth before them: and I knew not that she was the mother of them.

[13] I learned diligently, and do communicate her liberally: I do not hide her riches.

[14] For she is a treasure unto men that never faileth: which they that use become the friends of God, being commended for the gifts that come from learning.

[15] God hath granted me to speak as I would, and to conceive as is meet for the things that are given me: because it is he that leadeth unto wisdom, and directeth the wise.

[16] For in his hand are both we and our words; all wisdom also, and knowledge of workmanship.

[17] For he hath given me certain knowledge of the things that are, namely, to know how the world was made, and the operation of the elements:

[18] The beginning, ending, and midst of the times: the alterations of the turning of the sun, and the change of seasons:

[19] The circuits of years, and the positions of stars:

[20] The natures of living creatures, and the furies of wild beasts: the violence of winds, and the reasonings of men: the diversities of plants and the virtues of roots:

[21] And all such things as are either secret or manifest, them I know.

[22] For wisdom, which is the worker of all things, taught me: for in her is an understanding spirit holy, one only, manifold, subtil, lively, clear, undefiled, plain, not subject to hurt, loving the thing that is good quick, which cannot be letted, ready to do good,

[23] Kind to man, steadfast, sure, free from care, having all power, overseeing all things, and going through all understanding, pure, and most subtil, spirits.

[24] For wisdom is more moving than any motion: she passeth and goeth through all things by reason of her pureness.

[25] For she is the breath of the power of God, and a pure influence flowing from the glory of the Almighty: therefore can no defiled thing fall into her.

[26] For she is the brightness of the everlasting light, the unspotted mirror of the power of God, and the image of his goodness.

[27] And being but one, she can do all things: and remaining in herself, she maketh all things new: and in all ages entering into holy

souls, she maketh them friends of God, and prophets.

[28] For God loveth none but him that dwelleth with wisdom.

[29] For she is more beautiful than the sun, and above all the order of stars: being compared with the light, she is found before it.

[30] For after this cometh night: but vice shall not prevail against wisdom.

Wis.8

[1] Wisdom reacheth from one end to another mightily: and sweetly doth she order all things.

[2] I loved her, and sought her out from my youth, I desired to make her my spouse, and I was a lover of her beauty.

[3] In that she is conversant with God, she magnifieth her nobility: yea, the Lord of all things himself loved her.

[4] For she is privy to the mysteries of the knowledge of God, and a lover of his works.

[5] If riches be a possession to be desired in this life; what is richer than wisdom, that worketh all things?

[6] And if prudence work; who of all that are is a more cunning workman than she?

[7] And if a man love righteousness her labours are virtues: for she teacheth temperance and prudence, justice and fortitude: which are such things, as en can have nothing more profitable in their life.

[8] If a man desire much experience, she knoweth things of old, and conjectureth aright what is to come: she knoweth the subtilties of speeches, and can expound dark sentences: she foreseeth signs and wonders, and the events of seasons and times.

[9] Therefore I purposed to take her to me to live with me, knowing that she would be a

counsellor of good things, and a comfort in cares and grief.

[10] For her sake I shall have estimation among the multitude, and honour with the elders, though I be young.

[11] I shall be found of a quick conceit in judgment, and shall be admired in the sight of great men.

[12] When I hold my tongue, they shall bide my leisure, and when I speak, they shall give good ear unto me: if I talk much, they shall lay their hands upon their mouth.

[13] Moreover by the means of her I shall obtain immortality, and leave behind me an everlasting memorial to them that come after me.

[14] I shall set the people in order, and the nations shall be subject unto me.

[15] Horrible tyrants shall be afraid, when they do but hear of me; I shall be found good among the multitude, and valiant in war.

[16] After I am come into mine house, I will repose myself with her: for her conversation hath no bitterness; and to live with her hath no sorrow, but mirth and joy.

[17] Now when I considered these things in myself, and pondered them in my heart, how that to be allied unto wisdom is immortality;

[18] And great pleasure it is to have her friendship; and in the works of her hands are infinite riches; and in the exercise of

conference with her, prudence; and in talking with her, a good report; I went about seeking how to take her to me.

[19] For I was a witty child, and had a good spirit.

[20] Yea rather, being good, I came into a body undefiled.

[21] Nevertheless, when I perceived that I could not otherwise obtain her, except God gave her me; and that was a point of wisdom also to know whose gift she was; I prayed unto the Lord, and besought him, and with my whole heart I said,

Wis.9

[1] O God of my fathers, and Lord of mercy, who hast made all things with thy word,

[2] And ordained man through thy wisdom, that he should have dominion over the creatures which thou hast made,

[3] And order the world according to equity and righteousness, and execute judgment with an upright heart:

[4] Give me wisdom, that sitteth by thy throne; and reject me not from among thy children:

[5] For I thy servant and son of thine handmaid am a feeble person, and of a short time, and too young for the understanding of judgment and laws.

[6] For though a man be never so perfect among the children of men, yet if thy wisdom be not with him, he shall be nothing regarded.

[7] Thou hast chosen me to be a king of thy people, and a judge of thy sons and daughters:

[8] Thou hast commanded me to build a temple upon thy holy mount, and an altar in the city wherein thou dwellest, a resemblance of the holy tabernacle, which thou hast prepared from the beginning.

[9] And wisdom was with thee: which knoweth thy works, and was present when thou madest the world, and knew what was

acceptable in thy sight, and right in thy commandments.

[10] O send her out of thy holy heavens, and from the throne of thy glory, that being present she may labour with me, that I may know what is pleasing unto thee.

[11] For she knoweth and understandeth all things, and she shall lead me soberly in my doings, and preserve me in her power.

[12] So shall my works be acceptable, and then shall I judge thy people righteously, and be worthy to sit in my father's seat.

[13] For what man is he that can know the counsel of God? or who can think what the will of the Lord is?

[14] For the thoughts of mortal men are miserable, and our devices are but uncertain.

[15] For the corruptible body presseth down the soul, and the earthy tabernacle weigheth down the mind that museth upon many things.

[16] And hardly do we guess aright at things that are upon earth, and with labour do we find the things that are before us: but the things that are in heaven who hath searched out?

[17] And thy counsel who hath known, except thou give wisdom, and send thy Holy Spirit from above?

[18] For so the ways of them which lived on the earth were reformed, and men were taught

the things that are pleasing unto thee, and were saved through wisdom.

Wis.10

[1] She preserved the first formed father of the world, that was created alone, and brought him out of his fall,

[2] And gave him power to rule all things.

[3] But when the unrighteous went away from her in his anger, he perished also in the fury wherewith he murdered his brother.

[4] For whose cause the earth being drowned with the flood, wisdom again preserved it, and directed the course of the righteous in a piece of wood of small value.

[5] Moreover, the nations in their wicked conspiracy being confounded, she found out the righteous, and preserved him blameless unto God, and kept him strong against his tender compassion toward his son.

[6] When the ungodly perished, she delivered the righteous man, who fled from the fire which fell down upon the five cities.

[7] Of whose wickedness even to this day the waste land that smoketh is a testimony, and plants bearing fruit that never come to ripeness: and a standing pillar of salt is a monument of an unbelieving soul.

[8] For regarding not wisdom, they gat not only this hurt, that they knew not the things which were good; but also left behind them to the world a memorial of their foolishness: so

that in the things wherein they offended they could not so much as be hid.

[9] Rut wisdom delivered from pain those that attended upon her.

[10] When the righteous fled from his brother's wrath she guided him in right paths, shewed him the kingdom of God, and gave him knowledge of holy things, made him rich in his travels, and multiplied the fruit of his labours.

[11] In the covetousness of such as oppressed him she stood by him, and made him rich.

[12] She defended him from his enemies, and kept him safe from those that lay in wait, and in a sore conflict she gave him the victory; that he might know that goodness is stronger than all.

[13] When the righteous was sold, she forsook him not, but delivered him from sin: she went down with him into the pit,

[14] And left him not in bonds, till she brought him the sceptre of the kingdom, and power against those that oppressed him: as for them that had accused him, she shewed them to be liars, and gave him perpetual glory.

[15] She delivered the righteous people and blameless seed from the nation that oppressed them.

[16] She entered into the soul of the servant of the Lord, and withstood dreadful kings in wonders and signs;

[17] Rendered to the righteous a reward of their labours, guided them in a marvellous way, and was unto them for a cover by day, and a light of stars in the night season;

[18] Brought them through the Red sea, and led them through much water:

[19] But she drowned their enemies, and cast them up out of the bottom of the deep.

[20] Therefore the righteous spoiled the ungodly, and praised thy holy name, O Lord, and magnified with one accord thine hand, that fought for them.

[21] For wisdom opened the mouth of the dumb, and made the tongues of them that cannot speak eloquent.

Wis.11

[1] She prospered their works in the hand of the holy prophet.

[2] They went through the wilderness that was not inhabited, and pitched tents in places where there lay no way.

[3] They stood against their enemies, and were avenged of their adversaries.

[4] When they were thirsty, they called upon thee, and water was given them out of the flinty rock, and their thirst was quenched out of the hard stone.

[5] For by what things their enemies were punished, by the same they in their need were benefited.

[6] For instead of of a perpetual running river troubled with foul blood,

[7] For a manifest reproof of that commandment, whereby the infants were slain, thou gavest unto them abundance of water by a means which they hoped not for:

[8] Declaring by that thirst then how thou hadst punished their adversaries.

[9] For when they were tried albeit but in mercy chastised, they knew how the ungodly were judged in wrath and tormented, thirsting in another manner than the just.

[10] For these thou didst admonish and try, as a father: but the other, as a severe king, thou didst condemn and punish.

[11] Whether they were absent or present, they were vexed alike.

[12] For a double grief came upon them, and a groaning for the remembrance of things past.

[13] For when they heard by their own punishments the other to be benefited, they had some feeling of the Lord.

[14] For whom they respected with scorn, when he was long before thrown out at the casting forth of the infants, him in the end, when they saw what came to pass, they admired.

[15] But for the foolish devices of their wickedness, wherewith being deceived they worshipped serpents void of reason, and vile beasts, thou didst send a multitude of unreasonable beasts upon them for vengeance;

[16] That they might know, that wherewithal a man sinneth, by the same also shall he be punished.

[17] For thy Almighty hand, that made the world of matter without form, wanted not means to send among them a multitude of bears or fierce lions,

[18] Or unknown wild beasts, full of rage, newly created, breathing out either a fiery vapour, or filthy scents of scattered smoke, or shooting horrible sparkles out of their eyes:

[19] Whereof not only the harm might dispatch them at once, but also the terrible sight utterly destroy them.

[20] Yea, and without these might they have fallen down with one blast, being persecuted of vengeance, and scattered abroad through the breath of thy power: but thou hast ordered all things in measure and number and weight.

[21] For thou canst shew thy great strength at all times when thou wilt; and who may withstand the power of thine arm?

[22] For the whole world before thee is as a little grain of the balance, yea, as a drop of the morning dew that falleth down upon the earth.

[23] But thou hast mercy upon all; for thou canst do all things, and winkest at the sins of men, because they should amend.

[24] For thou lovest all the things that are, and abhorrest nothing which thou hast made: for never wouldest thou have made any thing, if thou hadst hated it.

[25] And how could any thing have endured, if it had not been thy will? or been preserved, if not called by thee?

[26] But thou sparest all: for they are thine, O Lord, thou lover of souls.

Wis. 12

[1] For thine incorruptible Spirit is in all things.

[2] Therefore chastenest thou them by little and little that offend, and warnest them by putting them in remembrance wherein they have offended, that leaving their wickedness they may believe on thee, O Lord.

[3] For it was thy will to destroy by the hands of our fathers both those old inhabitants of thy holy land,

[4] Whom thou hatedst for doing most odious works of witchcrafts, and wicked sacrifices;

[5] And also those merciless murderers of children, and devourers of man's flesh, and the feasts of blood,

[6] With their priests out of the midst of their idolatrous crew, and the parents, that killed with their own hands souls destitute of help:

[7] That the land, which thou esteemedst above all other, might receive a worthy colony of God's children.

[8] Nevertheless even those thou sparedst as men, and didst send wasps, forerunners of thine host, to destroy them by little and little.

[9] Not that thou wast unable to bring the ungodly under the hand of the righteous in battle, or to destroy them at once with cruel beasts, or with one rough word:

[10] But executing thy judgments upon them by little and little, thou gavest them place of repentance, not being ignorant that they were a naughty generation, and that their malice was bred in them, and that their cogitation would never be changed.

[11] For it was a cursed seed from the beginning; neither didst thou for fear of any man give them pardon for those things wherein they sinned.

[12] For who shall say, What hast thou done? or who shall withstand thy judgment? or who shall accuse thee for the nations that perish, whom thou made? or who shall come to stand against thee, to be revenged for the unrighteous men?

[13] For neither is there any God but thou that careth for all, to whom thou mightest shew that thy judgment is not unright.

[14] Neither shall king or tyrant be able to set his face against thee for any whom thou hast punished.

[15] Forsomuch then as thou art righteous thyself, thou orderest all things righteously: thinking it not agreeable with thy power to condemn him that hath not deserved to be punished.

[16] For thy power is the beginning of righteousness, and because thou art the Lord of all, it maketh thee to be gracious unto all.

[17] For when men will not believe that thou art of a full power, thou shewest thy strength, and among them that know it thou makest their boldness manifest.

[18] But thou, mastering thy power, judgest with equity, and orderest us with great favour: for thou mayest use power when thou wilt.

[19] But by such works hast thou taught thy people that the just man should be merciful, and hast made thy children to be of a good hope that thou givest repentance for sins.

[20] For if thou didst punish the enemies of thy children, and the condemned to death, with such deliberation, giving them time and place, whereby they might be delivered from their malice:

[21] With how great circumspection didst thou judge thine own sons, unto whose fathers thou hast sworn, and made covenants of good promises?

[22] Therefore, whereas thou dost chasten us, thou scourgest our enemies a thousand times more, to the intent that, when we judge, we should carefully think of thy goodness, and when we ourselves are judged, we should look for mercy.

[23] Wherefore, whereas men have lived dissolutely and unrighteously, thou hast tormented them with their own abominations.

[24] For they went astray very far in the ways of error, and held them for gods, which even among the beasts of their enemies were despised, being deceived, as children of no understanding.

[25] Therefore unto them, as to children without the use of reason, thou didst send a judgment to mock them.

[26] But they that would not be reformed by that correction, wherein he dallied with them, shall feel a judgment worthy of God.

[27] For, look, for what things they grudged, when they were punished, that is, for them whom they thought to be gods; [now] being punished in them, when they saw it, they acknowledged him to be the true God, whom before they denied to know: and therefore came extreme damnation upon them.

Wis.13

[1] Surely vain are all men by nature, who are ignorant of God, and could not out of the good things that are seen know him that is: neither by considering the works did they acknowledge the workmaster;

[2] But deemed either fire, or wind, or the swift air, or the circle of the stars, or the violent water, or the lights of heaven, to be the gods which govern the world.

[3] With whose beauty if they being delighted took them to be gods; let them know how much better the Lord of them is: for the first author of beauty hath created them.

[4] But if they were astonished at their power and virtue, let them understand by them, how much mightier he is that made them.

[5] For by the greatness and beauty of the creatures proportionably the maker of them is seen.

[6] But yet for this they are the less to be blamed: for they peradventure err, seeking God, and desirous to find him.

[7] For being conversant in his works they search him diligently, and believe their sight: because the things are beautiful that are seen.

[8] Howbeit neither are they to be pardoned.

[9] For if they were able to know so much, that they could aim at the world; how did they not sooner find out the Lord thereof?

[10] But miserable are they, and in dead things is their hope, who call them gods, which are the works of men's hands, gold and silver, to shew art in, and resemblances of beasts, or a stone good for nothing, the work of an ancient hand.

[11] Now a carpenter that felleth timber, after he hath sawn down a tree meet for the purpose, and taken off all the bark skilfully round about, and hath wrought it handsomely, and made a vessel thereof fit for the service of man's life;

[12] And after spending the refuse of his work to dress his meat, hath filled himself;

[13] And taking the very refuse among those which served to no use, being a crooked piece of wood, and full of knots, hath carved it diligently, when he had nothing else to do, and formed it by the skill of his understanding, and fashioned it to the image of a man;

[14] Or made it like some vile beast, laying it over with vermilion, and with paint colouring it red, and covering every spot therein;

[15] And when he had made a convenient room for it, set it in a wall, and made it fast with iron:

[16] For he provided for it that it might not fall, knowing that it was unable to help itself; for it is an image, and hath need of help:

[17] Then maketh he prayer for his goods, for his wife and children, and is not ashamed to speak to that which hath no life.

[18] For health he calleth upon that which is weak: for life prayeth to that which is dead; for aid humbly beseecheth that which hath least means to help: and for a good journey he asketh of that which cannot set a foot forward:

[19] And for gaining and getting, and for good success of his hands, asketh ability to do of him, that is most unable to do any thing.

Wis.14

[1] Again, one preparing himself to sail, and about to pass through the raging waves, calleth upon a piece of wood more rotten than the vessel that carrieth him.

[2] For verily desire of gain devised that, and the workman built it by his skill.

[3] But thy providence, O Father, governeth it: for thou hast made a way in the sea, and a safe path in the waves;

[4] Shewing that thou canst save from all danger: yea, though a man went to sea without art.

[5] Nevertheless thou wouldest not that the works of thy wisdom should be idle, and therefore do men commit their lives to a small piece of wood, and passing the rough sea in a weak vessel are saved.

[6] For in the old time also, when the proud giants perished, the hope of the world governed by thy hand escaped in a weak vessel, and left to all ages a seed of generation.

[7] For blessed is the wood whereby righteousness cometh.

[8] But that which is made with hands is cursed, as well it, as he that made it: he, because he made it; and it, because, being corruptible, it was called god.

[9] For the ungodly and his ungodliness are both alike hateful unto God.

[10] For that which is made shall be punished together with him that made it.

[11] Therefore even upon the idols of the Gentiles shall there be a visitation: because in the creature of God they are become an abomination, and stumblingblocks to the souls of men, and a snare to the feet of the unwise.

[12] For the devising of idols was the beginning of spiritual fornication, and the invention of them the corruption of life.

[13] For neither were they from the beginning, neither shall they be for ever.

[14] For by the vain glory of men they entered into the world, and therefore shall they come shortly to an end.

[15] For a father afflicted with untimely mourning, when he hath made an image of his child soon taken away, now honoured him as a god, which was then a dead man, and delivered to those that were under him ceremonies and sacrifices.

[16] Thus in process of time an ungodly custom grown strong was kept as a law, and graven images were worshipped by the commandments of kings.

[17] Whom men could not honour in presence, because they dwelt far off, they took the counterfeit of his visage from far, and made an express image of a king whom they honoured, to the end that by this their

forwardness they might flatter him that was absent, as if he were present.

[18] Also the singular diligence of the artificer did help to set forward the ignorant to more superstition.

[19] For he, peradventure willing to please one in authority, forced all his skill to make the resemblance of the best fashion.

[20] And so the multitude, allured by the grace of the work, took him now for a god, which a little before was but honoured.

[21] And this was an occasion to deceive the world: for men, serving either calamity or tyranny, did ascribe unto stones and stocks the incommunicable name.

[22] Moreover this was not enough for them, that they erred in the knowledge of God; but whereas they lived in the great war of ignorance, those so great plagues called they peace.

[23] For whilst they slew their children in sacrifices, or used secret ceremonies, or made revellings of strange rites;

[24] They kept neither lives nor marriages any longer undefiled: but either one slew another traiterously, or grieved him by adultery.

[25] So that there reigned in all men without exception blood, manslaughter, theft, and dissimulation, corruption, unfaithfulness, tumults, perjury,

[26] Disquieting of good men, forgetfulness of good turns, defiling of souls, changing of kind, disorder in marriages, adultery, and shameless uncleanness.

[27] For the worshipping of idols not to be named is the beginning, the cause, and the end, of all evil.

[28] For either they are mad when they be merry, or prophesy lies, or live unjustly, or else lightly forswear themselves.

[29] For insomuch as their trust is in idols, which have no life; though they swear falsely, yet they look not to be hurt.

[30] Howbeit for both causes shall they be justly punished: both because they thought not well of God, giving heed unto idols, and also unjustly swore in deceit, despising holiness.

[31] For it is not the power of them by whom they swear: but it is the just vengeance of sinners, that punisheth always the offence of the ungodly.

Wis.15

[1] But thou, O God, art gracious and true, longsuffering, and in mercy ordering all things,

[2] For if we sin, we are thine, knowing thy power: but we will not sin, knowing that we are counted thine.

[3] For to know thee is perfect righteousness: yea, to know thy power is the root of immortality.

[4] For neither did the mischievous invention of men deceive us, nor an image spotted with divers colours, the painter's fruitless labour;

[5] The sight whereof enticeth fools to lust after it, and so they desire the form of a dead image, that hath no breath.

[6] Both they that make them, they that desire them, and they that worship them, are lovers of evil things, and are worthy to have such things to trust upon.

[7] For the potter, tempering soft earth, fashioneth every vessel with much labour for our service: yea, of the same clay he maketh both the vessels that serve for clean uses, and likewise also all such as serve to the contrary: but what is the use of either sort, the potter himself is the judge.

[8] And employing his labours lewdly, he maketh a vain god of the same clay, even he which a little before was made of earth

himself, and within a little while after returneth to the same, out when his life which was lent him shall be demanded.

[9] Notwithstanding his care is, not that he shall have much labour, nor that his life is short: but striveth to excel goldsmiths and silversmiths, and endeavoureth to do like the workers in brass, and counteth it his glory to make counterfeit things.

[10] His heart is ashes, his hope is more vile than earth, and his life of less value than clay:

[11] Forasmuch as he knew not his Maker, and him that inspired into him an active soul, and breathed in a living spirit.

[12] But they counted our life a pastime, and our time here a market for gain: for, say they, we must be getting every way, though it be by evil means.

[13] For this man, that of earthly matter maketh brittle vessels and graven images, knoweth himself to offend above all others.

[14] And all the enemies of thy people, that hold them in subjection, are most foolish, and are more miserable than very babes.

[15] For they counted all the idols of the heathen to be gods: which neither have the use of eyes to see, nor noses to draw breath, nor ears to hear, nor fingers of hands to handle; and as for their feet, they are slow to go.

[16] For man made them, and he that borrowed his own spirit fashioned them: but no man can make a god like unto himself.

[17] For being mortal, he worketh a dead thing with wicked hands: for he himself is better than the things which he worshippeth: whereas he lived once, but they never.

[18] Yea, they worshipped those beasts also that are most hateful: for being compared together, some are worse than others.

[19] Neither are they beautiful, so much as to be desired in respect of beasts: but they went without the praise of God and his blessing.

Wis. 16

[1] Therefore by the like were they punished worthily, and by the multitude of beasts tormented.

[2] Instead of which punishment, dealing graciously with thine own people, thou preparedst for them meat of a strange taste, even quails to stir up their appetite:

[3] To the end that they, desiring food, might for the ugly sight of the beasts sent among them lothe even that, which they must needs desire; but these, suffering penury for a short space, might be made partakers of a strange taste.

[4] For it was requisite, that upon them exercising tyranny should come penury, which they could not avoid: but to these it should only be shewed how their enemies were tormented.

[5] For when the horrible fierceness of beasts came upon these, and they perished with the stings of crooked serpents, thy wrath endured not for ever:

[6] But they were troubled for a small season, that they might be admonished, having a sign of salvation, to put them in remembrance of the commandment of thy law.

[7] For he that turned himself toward it was not saved by the thing that he saw, but by thee, that art the Saviour of all.

[8] And in this thou madest thine enemies confess, that it is thou who deliverest from all evil:

[9] For them the bitings of grasshoppers and flies killed, neither was there found any remedy for their life: for they were worthy to be punished by such.

[10] But thy sons not the very teeth of venomous dragons overcame: for thy mercy was ever by them, and healed them.

[11] For they were pricked, that they should remember thy words; and were quickly saved, that not falling into deep forgetfulness, they might be continually mindful of thy goodness.

[12] For it was neither herb, nor mollifying plaister, that restored them to health: but thy word, O Lord, which healeth all things.

[13] For thou hast power of life and death: thou leadest to the gates of hell, and bringest up again.

[14] A man indeed killeth through his malice: and the spirit, when it is gone forth, returneth not; neither the soul received up cometh again.

[15] But it is not possible to escape thine hand.

[16] For the ungodly, that denied to know thee, were scourged by the strength of thine arm: with strange rains, hails, and showers, were they persecuted, that they could not avoid, and through fire were they consumed.

[17] For, which is most to be wondered at, the fire had more force in the water, that quencheth all things: for the world fighteth for the righteous.

[18] For sometime the flame was mitigated, that it might not burn up the beasts that were sent against the ungodly; but themselves might see and perceive that they were persecuted with the judgment of God.

[19] And at another time it burneth even in the midst of water above the power of fire, that it might destroy the fruits of an unjust land.

[20] Instead whereof thou feddest thine own people with angels' food, and didst send them from heaven bread prepared without their labour, able to content every man's delight, and agreeing to every taste.

[21] For thy sustenance declared thy sweetness unto thy children, and serving to the appetite of the eater, tempered itself to every man's liking.

[22] But snow and ice endured the fire, and melted not, that they might know that fire burning in the hail, and sparkling in the rain, did destroy the fruits of the enemies.

[23] But this again did even forget his own strength, that the righteous might be nourished.

[24] For the creature that serveth thee, who art the Maker increaseth his strength against

the unrighteous for their punishment, and abateth his strength for the benefit of such as put their trust in thee.

[25] Therefore even then was it altered into all fashions, and was obedient to thy grace, that nourisheth all things, according to the desire of them that had need:

[26] That thy children, O Lord, whom thou lovest, might know, that it is not the growing of fruits that nourisheth man: but that it is thy word, which preserveth them that put their trust in thee.

[27] For that which was not destroyed of the fire, being warmed with a little sunbeam, soon melted away:

[28] That it might be known, that we must prevent the sun to give thee thanks, and at the dayspring pray unto thee.

[29] For the hope of the unthankful shall melt away as the winter's hoar frost, and shall run away as unprofitable water.

Wis. 17

[1] For great are thy judgments, and cannot be expressed: therefore unnurtured souls have erred.

[2] For when unrighteous men thought to oppress the holy nation; they being shut up in their houses, the prisoners of darkness, and fettered with the bonds of a long night, lay [there] exiled from the eternal providence.

[3] For while they supposed to lie hid in their secret sins, they were scattered under a dark veil of forgetfulness, being horribly astonished, and troubled with [strange] apparitions.

[4] For neither might the corner that held them keep them from fear: but noises [as of waters] falling down sounded about them, and sad visions appeared unto them with heavy countenances.

[5] No power of the fire might give them light: neither could the bright flames of the stars endure to lighten that horrible night.

[6] Only there appeared unto them a fire kindled of itself, very dreadful: for being much terrified, they thought the things which they saw to be worse than the sight they saw not.

[7] As for the illusions of art magick, they were put down, and their vaunting in wisdom was reproved with disgrace.

[8] For they, that promised to drive away terrors and troubles from a sick soul, were sick themselves of fear, worthy to be laughed at.

[9] For though no terrible thing did fear them; yet being scared with beasts that passed by, and hissing of serpents,

[10] They died for fear, denying that they saw the air, which could of no side be avoided.

[11] For wickedness, condemned by her own witness, is very timorous, and being pressed with conscience, always forecasteth grievous things.

[12] For fear is nothing else but a betraying of the succours which reason offereth.

[13] And the expectation from within, being less, counteth the ignorance more than the cause which bringeth the torment.

[14] But they sleeping the same sleep that night, which was indeed intolerable, and which came upon them out of the bottoms of inevitable hell,

[15] Were partly vexed with monstrous apparitions, and partly fainted, their heart failing them: for a sudden fear, and not looked for, came upon them.

[16] So then whosoever there fell down was straitly kept, shut up in a prison without iron bars,

[17] For whether he were husbandman, or shepherd, or a labourer in the field, he was overtaken, and endured that necessity, which

could not be avoided: for they were all bound with one chain of darkness.

[18] Whether it were a whistling wind, or a melodious noise of birds among the spreading branches, or a pleasing fall of water running violently,

[19] Or a terrible sound of stones cast down, or a running that could not be seen of skipping beasts, or a roaring voice of most savage wild beasts, or a rebounding echo from the hollow mountains; these things made them to swoon for fear.

[20] For the whole world shined with clear light, and none were hindered in their labour:

[21] Over them only was spread an heavy night, an image of that darkness which should afterward receive them: but yet were they unto themselves more grievous than the darkness.

Wis.18

[1] Nevertheless thy saints had a very great light, whose voice they hearing, and not seeing their shape, because they also had not suffered the same things, they counted them happy.

[2] But for that they did not hurt them now, of whom they had been wronged before, they thanked them, and besought them pardon for that they had been enemies.

[3] Instead whereof thou gavest them a burning pillar of fire, both to be a guide of the unknown journey, and an harmless sun to entertain them honourably.

[4] For they were worthy to be deprived of light and imprisoned in darkness, who had kept thy sons shut up, by whom the uncorrupt light of the law was to be given unto the world.

[5] And when they had determined to slay the babes of the saints, one child being cast forth, and saved, to reprove them, thou tookest away the multitude of their children, and destroyedst them altogether in a mighty water.

[6] Of that night were our fathers certified afore, that assuredly knowing unto what oaths they had given credence, they might afterwards be of good cheer.

[7] So of thy people was accepted both the salvation of the righteous, and destruction of the enemies.

[8] For wherewith thou didst punish our adversaries, by the same thou didst glorify us, whom thou hadst called.

[9] For the righteous children of good men did sacrifice secretly, and with one consent made a holy law, that the saints should be like partakers of the same good and evil, the fathers now singing out the songs of praise.

[10] But on the other side there sounded an ill according cry of the enemies, and a lamentable noise was carried abroad for children that were bewailed.

[11] The master and the servant were punished after one manner; and like as the king, so suffered the common person.

[12] So they all together had innumerable dead with one kind of death; neither were the living sufficient to bury them: for in one moment the noblest offspring of them was destroyed.

[13] For whereas they would not believe any thing by reason of the enchantments; upon the destruction of the firstborn, they acknowledged this people to be the sons of God.

[14] For while all things were in quiet silence, and that night was in the midst of her swift course,

[15] Thine Almighty word leaped down from heaven out of thy royal throne, as a fierce man of war into the midst of a land of destruction,

[16] And brought thine unfeigned commandment as a sharp sword, and standing up filled all things with death; and it touched the heaven, but it stood upon the earth.

[17] Then suddenly visions of horrible dreams troubled them sore, and terrors came upon them unlooked for.

[18] And one thrown here, and another there, half dead, shewed the cause of his death.

[19] For the dreams that troubled them did foreshew this, lest they should perish, and not know why they were afflicted.

[20] Yea, the tasting of death touched the righteous also, and there was a destruction of the multitude in the wilderness: but the wrath endured not long.

[21] For then the blameless man made haste, and stood forth to defend them; and bringing the shield of his proper ministry, even prayer, and the propitiation of incense, set himself against the wrath, and so brought the calamity to an end, declaring that he was thy servant.

[22] So he overcame the destroyer, not with strength of body, nor force of arms, but with a word subdued him that punished, alleging the oaths and covenants made with the fathers.

[23] For when the dead were now fallen down by heaps one upon another, standing between, he stayed the wrath, and parted the way to the living.

[24] For in the long garment was the whole world, and in the four rows of the stones was the glory of the fathers graven, and thy Majesty upon the daidem of his head.

[25] Unto these the destroyer gave place, and was afraid of them: for it was enough that they only tasted of the wrath.

Wis.19

[1] As for the ungodly, wrath came upon them without mercy unto the end: for he knew before what they would do;

[2] How that having given them leave to depart, and sent them hastily away, they would repent and pursue them.

[3] For whilst they were yet mourning and making lamentation at the graves of the dead, they added another foolish device, and pursued them as fugitives, whom they had intreated to be gone.

[4] For the destiny, whereof they were worthy, drew them unto this end, and made them forget the things that had already happened, that they might fulfil the punishment which was wanting to their torments:

[5] And that thy people might pass a wonderful way: but they might find a strange death.

[6] For the whole creature in his proper kind was fashioned again anew, serving the peculiar commandments that were given unto them, that thy children might be kept without hurt:

[7] As namely, a cloud shadowing the camp; and where water stood before, dry land appeared; and out of the Red sea a way without impediment; and out of the violent stream a green field:

[8] Wherethrough all the people went that were defended with thy hand, seeing thy marvellous strange wonders.

[9] For they went at large like horses, and leaped like lambs, praising thee, O Lord, who hadst delivered them.

[10] For they were yet mindful of the things that were done while they sojourned in the strange land, how the ground brought forth flies instead of cattle, and how the river cast up a multitude of frogs instead of fishes.

[11] But afterwards they saw a new generation of fowls, when, being led with their appetite, they asked delicate meats.

[12] For quails came up unto them from the sea for their contentment.

[13] And punishments came upon the sinners not without former signs by the force of thunders: for they suffered justly according to their own wickedness, insomuch as they used a more hard and hateful behaviour toward strangers.

[14] For the Sodomites did not receive those, whom they knew not when they came: but these brought friends into bondage, that had well deserved of them.

[15] And not only so, but peradventure some respect shall be had of those, because they used strangers not friendly:

[16] But these very grievously afflicted them, whom they had received with feastings, and

were already made partakers of the same laws with them.

[17] Therefore even with blindness were these stricken, as those were at the doors of the righteous man: when, being compassed about with horrible great darkness, every one sought the passage of his own doors.

[18] For the elements were changed in themselves by a kind of harmony, like as in a psaltery notes change the name of the tune, and yet are always sounds; which may well be perceived by the sight of the things that have been done.

[19] For earthly things were turned into watery, and the things, that before swam in the water, now went upon the ground.

[20] The fire had power in the water, forgetting his own virtue: and the water forgat his own quenching nature.

[21] On the other side, the flames wasted not the flesh of the corruptible living things, though they walked therein; neither melted they the icy kind of heavenly meat that was of nature apt to melt.

[22] For in all things, O Lord, thou didst magnify thy people, and glorify them, neither didst thou lightly regard them: but didst assist them in every time and place.